Sorry, Mrs. Gunnarson

I sat in Mrs. Gunnarson's classroom with sweat breaking out on my forehead. This was the moment I had been dreading.

We were back at school for a brand-new year, and the time had arrived for the annual oral report those of us at Kennelworth Middle School had come to know as "What I Did on My Summer Vacation." I was doomed. What the aliens had done prevented me—Theo Benford, the brain—from being able to give a decent oral report.

This year, Juanita Alvarez, who preceded me in Mrs. Gunnarson's roll book, told us all about her family's trip to Mexico City. I couldn't believe how prepared she was. She even had visual aids. She had a sombrero and a red and green man's outer garment called a *serape* that she wore as she talked. She was doing a fantastic job.

As Juanita finished, everyone turned around to gawk at me. Several were smirking, and I could almost read their thoughts: *Top that, brain boy!*

Not that they didn't like me, but you know how it is in school. Every once in a while, everyone likes to see the star quarterback drop the ball or the smart kid have a brain burp.

So I did my best to pull myself together. I stood up with a sinking heart and made my way to the front of the room. I carried my only visual aid in a brown paper grocery bag.

Mrs. Gunnarson was smiling at Juanita. "Your oral report was fascinating, dear," she said, as Juanita returned to her seat. Mrs. Gunnarson then gave me her full attention. "I've heard all about what an imaginative writer Theodore is, and I'm sure that he will do just as well orally. What can you tell us about your summer vacation, Theodore?" Mrs. Gunnarson commented.

Well, this was it. The butterflies in my stomach weren't only fluttering, but flipping, flapping, and dancing the fandango. I swallowed hard as twenty-four pairs of eyes stared at me, and at least twelve mouths smirked. I set my paper bag down and said, "Uh, I really don't know how to begin my oral report."

Aliens Abducted My Report

By Brad Strickland

Illustrated by David Opie

CELEBRATION PRESS
Pearson Learning Group

Contents

Wayne Wilberforce rolled his eyes. He knew very well that he wouldn't have to give his oral report for several days because his last name started with a *W*.

I concentrated. "Well, okay. I've read a lot of science fiction, so I suppose I could begin my report the way a sci-fi writer might start a book. 'Little did I realize that the summer camp at Lake Winnemagoochee was inhabited by beings from beyond the bounds of space and time. . . .'"

Wayne raised his hand and flapped it around. "Mrs. Gunnarson! Theo is making my brain hurt with all those big words!" Wayne got the big laugh he wanted and just sat there grinning at me.

"Wayne, we don't interrupt speakers," Mrs. Gunnarson reminded him sternly. "Still, Theodore, perhaps you can get to the point of your story."

"I'm trying, Mrs. Gunnarson," I said. "Okay, maybe a writer like Isaac Asimov would be more factual about the whole thing and might begin the story like this: 'The distance between Earth and the planet Saroni is somewhat more than 50 light-years. At a speed of 500 miles per hour, it would take a jetliner about 67 million years to cover the distance.'"

"Are we there yet?" Wayne whispered, just loud enough for me to hear him.

I ignored him, knowing his turn would come. "Or a funny writer like Douglas Adams might start by saying, 'Aliens from the planet Saroni are among the most agreeable beings in the known Universe. For example, they all agree that they don't much like humans and would like to see something awful happen to them.'"

Before Wayne had a chance to make another joke, Mrs. Gunnarson said, "Theodore, I admire the fact that you have read so many challenging books, but for this oral report, it might be better for you to just tell the story in your own way. Don't try to imitate Isaac Asimov or some other famous science fiction writer."

I felt my face turn hot and red. "I'm sorry, Mrs. Gunnarson. I knew this report would be coming up, so I tried to prepare. Really, I did. I even got my dad to give me his old laptop computer when he bought a new one. I was going to take notes and be ready for this report more than I've ever been ready for one in my life, but . . . "

"What, Theodore?"

I looked down at my shoes. "Aliens abducted my oral report, Mrs. Gunnarson."

Everyone laughed again. If I had been trying to be a comedian, it would have been a great moment.

Unfortunately, I didn't want to get all those laughs. In fact, I would have been grateful to just sit down at my desk again. However, this was a challenge, and I had to meet it. I gulped down my embarrassment and said, "You're right, Mrs. Gunnarson. I'll just have to tell the story my own way. Believe me, I know how crazy it all is going to sound, but hear me out and you'll see why this is so hard for me."

Then I took a deep breath and started to tell the whole weird story to a bunch of people who would never believe me in a billion years.

Chapter 2

Welcome to Lake Winnemagoochee

"I'm going to learn to ride a horse and learn to take care of a horse and swim and . . ."

That was my little sister, Maggie. It was a hot day in July, and we were on a bus with about 40 other kids, bouncing along a country road toward summer camp.

I tried to ignore Maggie. Dad had given me his old laptop computer, and I removed it from the case I kept it in. The airtight, waterproof case I used to house the superhero figures I'd collected when I was Maggie's age now kept the laptop safe.

I turned the laptop on and started playing *Objective: Proxima Centauri*, a space-race game in which you send your spaceship to the star Proxima Centauri, find a planet to colonize, and establish a working society. That requires a little concentration. It doesn't require your little sister constantly peeking over your shoulder saying, "What's the red guy doing? What's the green guy doing? Can I play?"

I finally turned off the laptop and returned it to its case. My main reason for having the computer wasn't really to play games, anyway but to be prepared for the expected and much anticipated "What I Did on My Summer Vacation" report that we'd have to present when school started again.

I stared out the bus window for half an hour, feeling sort of resentful. Ordinarily, I am not an outdoors kind of guy and stretching ahead of me were three solid weeks of summer camp.

Swimming is okay I guess, but I don't like to go hiking, and you can forget about horseback riding. Horses don't like me the way they do Maggie, and anyway, they smell funny.

We passed fields with grazing cows, pine forests, and a whole lot of practically nothing at all. We finally passed under the sign that read "Welcome to Lake Winnemagoochee." Then, with a squeal of brakes, the bus lurched to a stop in front of the big main cabin.

It hadn't changed since last year, and I even recognized two of the counselors, dressed in their ranger hats, brown short-sleeved uniform shirts, and tan shorts. The counselors were Chris and Wendy, who greeted us as we clambered off the bus, lugging our backpacks and duffel bags.

"Hi, Theo!" Chris said cheerfully. "Welcome back. This year we have your sister, too, right? Which one is she?"

Maggie waved, and Wendy said, "Okay! Come with me, Maggie, and I'll show you your cabin and your three cabinmates."

"Where are the horses?" asked Maggie, as she walked off with Wendy.

After Maggie left, I grabbed my backpack, duffel bag, and laptop computer and followed Chris. We passed the Tenderfoot cabins, and I realized that this year I was going to be in one of the Woodcraft cabins.

I liked that. The Tenderfoot cabins clustered close around the main part of the camp so if the little kids got scared, there were counselors close by to reassure them. The Woodcraft cabins were farther away at the edge of the woods because Woodcraft campers were older and unlikely to be scared by owl hoots.

Chris stopped in front of Woodcraft Cabin 3 and yelled, "Guys! Your last cabinmate is here!"

The door of the log cabin opened, and three guys spilled out. Chris introduced us. Rusty had reddish-brown hair and a big splash of freckles across his nose, and Franklin had straight black hair and a happy smile. Then, there was Eddie.

"Just call me ESP! That stands for my name, Edward Samuel Philips," Eddie exclaimed. "It also means that I can tell what you're thinking, and right now you're thinking you've never seen such an odd-looking kid in your life!"

That was just what I *was* thinking. ESP was a skinny kid, and for some reason his head looked really big. He had wispy hair, that was, well, green. His eyes were two different colors, and he was wearing a pair of swim fins.

"Now, you're wondering why my hair is green," ESP said happily. "I have a ready explanation for you. It's because of the chlorine in the pool! The chlorine has turned my hair *green*! Yes!"

"Come on in," Rusty said. "We saved the top bunk by the window for you because ESP said that's the one you'd want."

"Uh, thanks," I replied, a bit surprised. I *did* like the top bunk, and I *did* like to look out the window at night when I was in bed.

Soon, it was time for camp orientation. Franklin talked ESP into putting on some sneakers. ESP put the right shoe on his left foot and vice versa.

"Those are the wrong feet," Rusty said.

"Incorrect!" ESP replied with a laugh. "These are the only feet that I possess! It is a joke to make you laugh. Yes!" Then he changed the shoes to the other feet.

I rolled my eyes at ESP's humor. I hoped ESP wasn't reading my mind just then, because I was thinking I was happy to be in a bunk far from his.

We trooped along to the orientation meeting in the dining hall. The counselors gave us a pep talk, telling us how we were going to love swimming, fishing, horseback riding, and arts and crafts. They were so cheerful that it was hard not to get into the camp spirit, at least a little.

We had dinner right after orientation. We got our tray and went through the serving area to fill our plates. Everyone walked around with their tray, looking for a familiar face and a place to sit. I noticed that Rusty and Franklin took the last two seats at a table with other Woodcraft campers. *Tomorrow I'd better be quicker if I want to sit there*, I thought.

I ended up sitting with Maggie, who was dying to tell me about the horse she had seen wandering around by the stables. After going on and on for several minutes, barely stopping to take a breath, Maggie finally said, "I'm starving. Let's eat."

We looked down at the scary-looking camp food on our trays. Maggie poked at the grayish-brown slab on her plate. "What is this stuff?" she asked.

From all the way across the dining hall, ESP yelled, "What is the mystery of the mystery meat? It tastes okay, but it doesn't look neat! It's shaped like someone's dirty feet!"

I groaned. With ESP's lame jokes, it was going to be a long, long three weeks.

Chapter 3

There's a Foozlum in My Nimplog!

It had been a long day so when lights out time rolled around, I was ready to turn in. ESP wasn't sleepy, so I let him borrow my laptop so he could try my space-race game. He proceeded to have an argument with one of the cartoon men because he didn't think red was a respectful color for a starship pilot. After about ten minutes, ESP gave in when he said the cartoon figure told him the color matched his eyes. "Every nimplog has a right to color coordination," he said.

I was more tired than I thought. For a while, I tossed and turned, trying to get comfortable the way you do when you're in a strange place for the first night. My eyes were just about closed when I thought I heard a strange, whirring noise.

Too sleepy to raise my head up, I glanced at the window, which was a few feet away and was wide open to let in the cool night air. I saw ESP bend over, lean out the window, and float up into the air like a balloon.

I was so sleepy that my only thought was, *I hope ESP's not wearing those goofy swim fins*. Then I went to sleep but not for long.

Soon, my brain processed what I had seen, and I sat up in bed. *Hey, dummy, he just floated away!* My heart was pounding. "ESP!" I called out.

"Yes!" came his voice from the darkness. "You have had a strange dream." It hadn't seemed like a dream at all. It had to be, though. People just don't go floating off!

17

The next morning when I woke up, the first thing I thought about was my weird dream. However, I soon forgot about ESP floating because Chris took us on a nature hike.

I'd been on the hike before, but it was still kind of interesting. Chris found some heron tracks on the lakeshore, which were 6 inches long and looked as if they might have been left by a small dinosaur. Then Chris started to tell us about the kinds of animals and birds we might see, including opossums, skunks, and blue jays.

"What about a creepido?" asked ESP.

Everyone looked at him. ESP was wearing a camp T-shirt and shorts. He didn't look quite as odd as he had in an oversized shirt and swim fins, but he still looked pretty strange. Chris said, "A what?"

"Creepido! You know, it's partly like a bird because it flies through the air and partly like a whale because it swims. It hangs by its tail and whistles in the night."

Chris looked as if he thought ESP was joking. "I don't think there's any creepido around here," he said.

ESP saw the 11 other boys staring at him. "It is a joke. Yes! We laugh now. Ha, ha, ha," he said.

I don't mean he laughed. He said the words "ha, ha, ha" just as if he were saying, "I like milk."

Chris just stared at him and then said, "Come on, guys. I'll show you a duck's nest."

Rusty and I were straggling at the rear of the group. Rusty whispered, "Is he for real?"

"ESP?" I asked, as if Rusty could have been talking about anyone else. "Sometimes, I think he's just got a freaky sense of humor, and it's all a put-on. Other times, I think he's so far out there, you couldn't get his attention with a foghorn."

We finished our nature hike and wrote letters home. Afterward, I hauled out the laptop and started writing everything down. I made notes about all the odd things that ESP had done since I arrived at camp because I wanted to remember everything for my school report.

Soon, I found a file on the computer that I didn't recognize. It read: *To Saronian Command: Have infiltrated a Terran nimplog. Searching for foozlum. Agent . . .* and then some weird-looking symbols.

I started to ask Rusty to come and look at it, but the file erased itself. I stared at ESP, who was snoozing on his bunk. I wondered if he'd been fooling with my computer when he was arguing with the game because those words sounded like something he would make up.

Before long, it was time for lunch, and Maggie wanted to sit with me again. I really wanted to sit with the other guys from my cabin, but when I saw the pleading look on her face, I agreed.

She scarfed down her peanut butter and jelly sandwich, drank her milk in huge thirsty gulps, and didn't say a single word about horses, for a change. Instead, she asked, "Did the helicopter wake you up last night?"

"What helicopter?" I asked her.

"I saw it from my window. There was a round, bright light hanging right over your cabin. It made a funny sound, like . . ." Maggie rattled her tongue and made a noise like *whrrrrrrr*.

Goosebumps broke out on my arms. That was just what I had dreamed! A cold chill ran down my back, and then it plopped on my head.

"Sorry!" yelled ESP, right behind me.

I jumped up, swiping at the cold lump on my head. "I have dropped my iced-cream dessert, and it has landed in your hair. Yes!"

That took my mind off lights in the sky, whirring noises, and funny-looking floating kids. At least, it did for the moment.

All that day, I watched ESP, who tried to paddle a canoe with a tennis racket. When we made wallets in arts and crafts, he turned his into a goofy-looking hand puppet.

Later, Rusty, Franklin, ESP, and I walked to our cabin for lights out. ESP threw his arms over all our shoulders and said, "We have a resourceful and amiable nimplog. Yes!"

"What is a *nimplog*?" asked Franklin.

ESP blinked his buggy eyes. "A nimplog! A group of us all working together, you know, and being happy."

Nimplog was one of the strange words I'd found on the laptop. It reminded me of the other peculiar word I had seen there. I leaned toward Rusty and whispered, "Don't look now, but I think there's a foozlum in my nimplog."

Rusty laughed and said, "Now, you sound just like someone else I know, and that's pretty scary!"

ESP, however, gasped and jumped about two feet into the air, and then he stared at me for what seemed like five minutes. I don't think he could have heard what I'd whispered, but then his nickname was ESP.

Of course, I didn't know it at the time, but the fun was just getting started. Nimplogs and foozlums were just the beginning of this crazy adventure.

Chapter 4

Aliens Took My Sister but Left the Broccoli!

If I had any dreams that night, I couldn't remember them the next morning. ESP kept giving me puzzled glances as we lined up for breakfast. I saw Maggie already in line and went over to speak to her. "So how was horseback riding yesterday?" I asked her.

Maggie stared at me for several seconds as if I'd grown a second head. Then I thought I heard a faint click. "Theodore! How are you? You are . . . my brother," she said, sounding rather odd. "I hope you are enjoying your camping experience."

Goosebumps began to parade up my arms. It was obvious that something was definitely wrong here. I knew it was something serious when Maggie loaded up her tray with oatmeal because she never eats oatmeal.

ESP came up and clapped me on the shoulder. "Today we eat together and share funny stories and nourishment. Yes!"

Maggie gave him a fake little smile and drifted away. ESP practically dragged me through the serving line. When we sat down, I discovered he had put a waffle, a hard-boiled egg, and a piece of bacon on my tray and had covered it all with oatmeal. He had a similar plate, and he dug in with enthusiasm.

"Yes! Lots of vitamins and minerals, with protein," said ESP. He held up his hard-boiled egg, dripping sad little plops of oatmeal.

"Chickens come from these, yes? What sort of soil is best for planting them in?" he asked.

ESP chattered away, but I ignored him because, at the moment, I was much more interested in what was going on with Maggie. She left the dining hall with some of the other girls, and I stared after her, hoping that the peculiar mood that had come over my little sister wasn't permanent.

All morning long, I continued to worry. We had horseback-riding lessons, and as we strapped on our helmets, I wondered if maybe Maggie had fallen off a horse onto her head or something.

My horse was a gray mare with black spots called Stipple. She seemed gentle enough, but she shied away whenever ESP came close, not that I blamed her. I was starting to wish that I could keep my distance from him, too.

I was anxious to find Maggie at lunchtime, but I couldn't spot her anywhere in the crowded dining hall. ESP stuck to me the way warts stick to a frog, and this time *he* was the one who seemed distracted. When we sat down, he looked at his plate and jumped up out of his chair, his already buggy eyes bulging. "What is this?"

Franklin, who was sitting beside him, looked over at his tray. "That's broccoli," he said. "It's supposed to be good for you, but I think it's pretty yucky. I sure wouldn't get a whole plateful of it the way you've done."

ESP reached out a shaky hand and picked up one little limp stalk of broccoli. "Have they cooked you?" he wailed. "Are you still conscious? Can you speak to me?"

"It's a vegetable, ESP," Rusty said with irritation in his voice. "It doesn't talk."

"A vegetable?" ESP stared at the floppy piece of broccoli. "Oh, yes, I see, no eyes or mouth. What a relief! It looked just like the brushy-headed people of Chisnillit, the great green glowing planet in the Hoomballa System."

A silence of about half a minute followed. I think we were all just trying to ignore ESP's latest peculiar outburst.

Finally, Rusty asked me, "What's wrong with you, man? You're not eating your burger."

"My sister's acting creepy," I told him.

Franklin shrugged. "Yeah, well, little sisters are usually pretty creepy," he observed.

"Not creepy like this. She's acting as if she's not herself at all, like she doesn't even know me."

ESP jerked his head to look at us. "What? Your sister acts as if she doesn't know you? Would you say she acts as if she were a different person?"

"Sort of," I admitted reluctantly. "I don't even think she recognized me this morning."

ESP jumped up, ran around the table, and practically dragged me out the door. "Come! Come! We must discuss this at once! Hurry!"

He pulled me to our cabin. Once inside, he stared nervously at my face, licked his lips a couple of times, and then said, "I have to trust you, I think. Last evening, you used a word I did not think you would know, the word *foozlum*. Where did you hear this word?"

"I didn't hear it. I read it," I told him. "It was on my computer screen when . . ."

"The lappy top! Resonance frequencies and crossover transmission of intentional meaning! Why did I not think of that before?" ESP ran to my locker, dragged out the carrying case that held the laptop, handed it to me, and said, "Take it out and turn it on, quickly!"

I fired it up. When I had a blank screen, he leaned back and closed his eyes.

I stared in disbelief as words appeared on the screen as if by magic: *To Saronian Command: Test transmission, please ignore.* The letters faded away. "How did you do that?" I asked.

"I have a transmission device for sending signals that are faster than light. Its frequency resonates with the lappy top, but that is not important now. No! Do you know what a foozlum is? No, I see in your mind you have ignorance, so I show you. Yes!" He dug out a rolled-up poster from his own locker and held it up. "This is a foozlum, see?"

The picture resembled someone's attempt to draw a robot armadillo with a satellite television antenna attached. Lines stretched out from the mechanical-looking thing in the center to the corners where there were pictures of a rabbit, a flying eagle, a broom, and, in the lower right corner, George Washington.

"Now is clear, yes?"

"Now is clear, no!" I shouted. "What in the world are you talking about, ESP?"

"Not in the world!" ESP muttered. "I have to tell you because there is no other way. I am not an ordinary human boy."

"You can say that again," I agreed. Of course, ESP repeated what he had just said.

"Prepare yourself for a mighty shock, Theo," ESP said. "I am not a human at all. I am a Saronian from the planet Saroni. Yes! I am an agent of the Galactic Bureau of Interspecies Affairs, and I am tracking down a rogue foozlum."

"Yes!" ESP continued. "The foozlum entered Earth's atmosphere and landed here at Lake Winnemagoochee. Now it has morphed, I think, to resemble your sister. Is all clear?"

"Look," I told him, "that's got to be the craziest story I have ever heard. Anyway, you still haven't told me what a foozlum is."

"Didn't you listen with your ears and see with your eyes? Is it supposed to be the other way around? No! I explain again that a foozlum is smart, but not living—a mechanical thing. Yes! Like the lappy top, but smarter. It can change itself to other forms, so it could take the shape of a George Washington or a broom or a bird or a . . . This is rabbit, yes?" He unrolled the poster and pointed.

"No, that's George Washington. The rabbit is up here."

"Rabbit, rabbit. Okay, rabbit could be robot because foozlum is robot and could be rabbit. Foozlum finds a new form and changes, so maybe now it has taken the form of your sister, Maggie person."

I jumped up, really alarmed. "What has it done to Maggie?"

ESP dropped the poster and patted my shoulders, pushing me into a chair and smiling in a faintly maniacal way. "No! No harm to her. She may be confused or lost somewhere, but no harm . . . no lasting harm! When foozlum change again, everything all right. Foozlum must be found! ESP must find it. Yes!"

ESP lowered his voice. "Others may be looking for foozlum, so you must not talk with others, human or else, about foozlum! Only talk to agent of the Galactic Bureau for Interspecies Affairs, and that is me, yes, ESP! Is deal for us two now, if I help find your real true sister, not your foozlum sister? Yes?"

I felt as if I'd been riding on a runaway roller coaster. "If I help you find the foozlum, then you'll help me find my sister. Right?"

"Correct! Yes!"

Well, what choice did I have? If I refused and went back home with the fake version of Maggie, our parents would notice sooner or later. If nothing else, they might notice that her table manners had improved. I gave up trying to make sense of anything and just said, "It's a deal."

Chapter 5

A Funny Thing Happened

The rest of that day, I searched for Maggie, but no one else seemed to miss her, which was weird. I mean, the counselors usually know exactly where the younger kids are. I didn't want to come right out and ask Wendy about Maggie because I had promised ESP to keep things to myself, so that left me wandering around peering into cabins.

ESP assured me he had a plan, but I didn't trust him. That night, I went to bed without undressing. I lay under my sheets and watched for anything odd.

A funny light began to glow outside around midnight. ESP slipped quietly out of bed. He floated out the window again, and I jumped down from the bunk and climbed out right after him.

I looked up and saw the helicopter that Maggie had mentioned—except it wasn't a helicopter, but a small hovering disk. It glowed with a bright blue-white light and made a high-pitched whirring sound.

I was hot on ESP's trail, as he ducked through the woods, came to an oak tree, and rapped on it as if he were knocking on a door. I know how hard this is to believe, but a door opened in that tree, a door spilling orange light out into the night. ESP stepped through and the door started to close, but before it did, I leaped through the closing gap.

I felt strange right away, and not just because the bright orange light half blinded me. I felt sort of bouncy, as if I were wading in shoulder-deep water. Somehow, I was standing on a thin metal platform attached to the side of a weird metal skyscraper, and I was far above the ground.

The ground was covered with bizarre-looking buildings. The things I saw in the distance might have been trees, but they looked deformed, and the sun was four times the size it should be and red besides. I almost bounced off the platform and just managed to grab a rail.

"You!" ESP yelled. "You should not have come through the transdimensional promotor! I am in trouble now. Yes!"

"You aren't the only one," I gasped. "Where on Earth are we?"

"Not on Earth! On my home planet, Saroni, except not really. Really we are inside the transdimensional promotor, and only our consciousnesses believe we are on Saroni. Yes!"

I couldn't argue with that, mainly because I couldn't understand it.

ESP shook his head. "Well, it cannot be helped. We will clear your memory of this later. Come, we must attend the Council and learn their advice! Yes!"

He led me through an arched doorway and into a round room where a dozen ESPs waited for us. At least, they looked enough like him to be related except that their hair was greener than his. Some of them yelped when they saw me, but ESP waved his hands. "This is Earth human called Theo here in transdimensional promotor! Human has interest in the foozlum. Yes!"

They jabbered at him in a language that sounded like a penguin shouting at a sea lion. Then, one of them waved some kind of odd device in the air, and suddenly, I could understand what they were saying: ". . . outrageous breach of confidentiality! You know better than this!"

ESP humbly replied, "I understand, fellow council members. However, this truly is an unusual case since the foozlum malfunctioned and landed on the wrong planet. The surface of that planet, I might add, is largely liquid, a hydrogen-oxygen compound that Earth's inhabitants call *water*."

"That's perfect," one of the ESP clones said. "This foozlum will dissolve in water! All you have to do is find it and . . ."

To my shock, I heard myself saying, "Me have strong objection. Yes! Is my sister person the foozlum now look like!" I stopped and glared at ESP. "What matter with my voice now?"

"It is the translation device," ESP said. "It is not perfect, as you may have noticed during my conversations with you on Earth. Now you are speaking our language, but imperfectly. I understand that it is somewhat embarrassing."

Quickly, ESP explained that the foozlum had taken the form of Maggie. We waited while the council members huddled together.

After only a few seconds, one of the council members said, "You two must work together to locate the foozlum. Yes! In exchange, we authorize our agent to make sure that no harm comes to the human called Maggie. Is that agreeable to you, human called Theo?"

"Yes! Agreeability is greatly appreciated!" At that moment, I decided that I'd never think ESP was talking weird again.

ESP argued for another few minutes about using something called a flux impedance detector. Finally, the council agreed to let him use it.

ESP grabbed my arm and dragged me through the arched door. I thought we were going to fall off the platform, but all at once, everything went dark. The next moment, we stumbled out of the tree into Camp Winnemagoochee.

"Good," ESP said. "Now I can use technology to track foozlum." He reached into the pocket of his pajamas and took out two things that looked like wristwatches. "Here! You wear one, and I wear one. If it flashes red, then foozlum is close by."

I strapped the device, which looked just like a watch, onto my wrist. The round face was dark, which meant that no foozlum was around.

I wasn't quite ready to track the foozlum. First, I wanted ESP to explain something he had said earlier after I had followed him through the transdimensional promotor. "What did you mean about 'clearing my memory?' I don't like the sound of that!"

ESP looked uncomfortable. "Must do this because no one on Earth can have any memory of foozlum. You won't lose whole memory. Remember about camp and school lessons. Yes! Just won't remember about me or foozlum."

"But I don't want anyone fooling around with my memory!" I objected.

"Is better that way. Yes! Only way for you not to forget it all would be . . ." He stopped.

Impatient, I said, "Keep talking. I want to hear this. How can I keep my memory?"

ESP shrugged. "When foozlum is captured, its last act is to clear memories. They fade away in an hour, then you cannot remember. Of course, foozlum could return your memory, but foozlum will be gone then. Yes! I will take it with me."

Reluctantly, I agreed, "Okay, as long as everything is back to normal."

ESP nodded, looking worried. "Is only one problem. Other species also look for foozlum, and we must not let them find it! Consequences could be very grave."

I didn't like that word. "What do you mean by 'grave'?"

ESP shrugged and said. "Maybe not so grave. Maybe if others find foozlum first, little bit of Earth still be left." He shrugged again. "Maybe."

Chapter 6

When Aliens Collide

I hardly slept at all that night, and the next morning, I was eager to find Maggie, or whatever it was impersonating Maggie. However, she wasn't in the dining hall for breakfast.

After breakfast we had a canoe lesson and then some free time before lunch to write letters home and relax. As soon as I could get away, I headed straight for the stables because I figured that if the substitute Maggie was posing as the real thing, she'd have to hang out with the horses.

Just my luck, the counselor everyone called "Hammer" because his name was Hamilton, was assigned to the stables that day. I won't say he was lazy, but he really seemed to get a lot of enjoyment out of watching other people work.

When he spotted me, he brightened right up. "Theo! The girls have just finished their horseback riding lesson, and now the horses need grooming, so grab a brush and pitch in!"

"Did you see my sister in the class?" I asked.

Hammer shook his head. "No, this was the older group. I haven't seen Maggie in a day or two. Okay, I've got something I need to do in my cabin, so you get busy with the horses."

Like take a nap, I thought.

I hurried through the chore of brushing the horses. Finally, I got to the last one, Stipple.

"Here you go," I said, leading the horse out of the stall so I could brush her well.

"I wish you could tell me where Maggie is."

"I wish I could, too."

A day or two earlier, my jaw would have dropped to the stable floor, but somehow after the tree, the transdimensional whatchamacallit, the foozlum, and ESP, a talking horse didn't shock me. "Let me guess," I said. "You're an alien."

"Brush my shoulder, please. I've been trying to reach that itch. Actually, I'm the agent of the Galactic Bureau of Interspecies Affairs."

"I thought that was ESP!"

"No! He is a Saronian! He is looking for—well, something."

"The foozlum," I said matter of factly. "I know all about it."

"The Saronians must not find the foozlum first!" Stipple told me firmly, stamping one foot. "I am a Ventirian. We are trying to prevent the Saronians from getting the foozlum because . . ."

I guessed, "Because you don't want them to have the technology?"

"Uh, right! It would be disastrous if the Saronians got the foozlum technology!"

"Well, the foozlum is my sister right now, and I have to find her."

"No, the foozlum has changed form again. It became aware of me yesterday and escaped, so I don't know what the foozlum is right now. It is important that we locate it immediately, so will you trust me, Theo?"

"After everything I've seen, I don't know who to trust anymore!" I groaned.

"Uh, Theo?" It was Franklin's voice, behind me. I whirled around and saw Franklin and Rusty staring at me curiously. I could almost read their minds: *This guy is as strange as ESP!*

I patted Stipple and led her back into the stall. "Good horsie," I heard myself saying. "Just finishing here. What's up, guys?"

"Your laptop is going crazy," Rusty said. "It's making all kinds of beeping sounds, so we thought you ought to know."

We hurried back to the cabin, and I hauled the laptop from under the bunk. It was beeping away, even though it was closed and powered down.

As soon as I opened it, words started to appear on the screen: *Theo, if you're there, answer me. This is Maggie.*

Rusty and Franklin peered over my shoulders as I typed, *Where are you?*

42

I'm not sure. Somehow, I'm, on a Ventirian spaceship in orbit around Earth, except they say I'm in the trans-something-or-other.

"You're not even hooked up to the Internet," Franklin said, his mouth hanging open in astonishment. "Unless . . . Is this a wireless deal?"

"It's weirder than that," I grunted and told Maggie to hang in there until I could get to her.

I sighed. "Okay, guys," I said. "I need your help."

I told them the whole story, but I'm not sure they believed me. Like me, they knew ESP, so by this time, not much would surprise them.

Chapter 7

Aliens, Go Home!

We couldn't do anything about Maggie until later that day. If the three of us just disappeared into the woods, someone would notice. Anyway, I had no idea how to open the tree, and I wasn't even sure if I could find it again.

After lunch, I hooked up with ESP again. We combed through Camp Winnemagoochee, looking for Maggie and the foozlum, but we didn't have any luck.

"You must be careful," ESP warned me. "Other species are looking for the foozlum, so do not let them trick you! If they find the foozlum before I do, things could work out very badly for us."

"Look," I said, "we can cover more ground if we split up. Why don't we meet back at the cabin before dinner? I'll take the stables and the dock, and you can take the nature trail and the dining hall. If one of us finds something, he can leave a message in the cabin."

So we cut swimming lessons and started searching. I didn't see anything interesting for a while, but then, outside the stable, I heard someone whistling. I hid behind a tree and saw Hammer walking along, coming back from the lake with a huge beach towel over his shoulder.

As soon as he passed my tree, the wristwatch device on my arm started flashing a bright red! *Hammer!* I thought to myself. *He's the foozlum!*

I had to determine very quickly if I should trust ESP or Stipple, and then I remembered that Maggie had said she had connected with the Ventiri. Stipple was one of those, so I headed into the stable.

"Stipple!" I said in the darkness. "I found the foozlum!"

"Theo, open the stall!" Stipple responded.

I did, and Stipple pranced out. I hastily told the horse about the finder device and how it had flashed when Hammer had passed by.

"Quickly!" Stipple shouted. "This is our chance!"

"Thank you! Yes!" said a voice behind me.

I whirled around and saw that ESP was closing the stable door. "Now the Saronians can capture the foozlum!"

I lurched forward, but he slammed the big door. I heard the bar outside drop into place. "We're trapped!"

"We cannot let the Saronians get to the foozlum first!" Stipple said urgently.

"Listen, your people have my sister caught in a tree, or on a spaceship, or something, and—"

"We are protecting her! Get us out of here, quickly."

The door was the only way out. I peeked through the crack between the door and the frame, and I could see the bar that held the door shut. *If I could just find something thin enough and strong enough to lift the bar!*

I searched and found a big flat shovel used for cleaning up after the horses, grabbed it, and shoved its blade through the crack. Using it as a lever, I worked the bar up and out of its latch and the door sprang open.

"Come on!" I shouted to Stipple.

Stipple and I ran out quickly, while the wrist device, once again, flashed incessantly. I looked up just in time to see a rabbit speed past us.

Right behind it was ESP yelling, "Stop it!"

Behind him, Hammer yelled, "Wait for me!" They zigged and zagged, disappearing down the riding trail in the direction of camp.

Stipple shouted, "Follow me!"

Following a horse is kind of hard since it's essentially four legs to two. Stipple got to the main building ahead of me where I heard people yelling.

"Hurry up!" the horse shouted.

Rusty and Franklin were pointing at Stipple.

"That horse talked!"

"You're hearing things!" I yelled.

As I caught up, I saw something leap into the air and sprout huge wings. For a second, it looked like a metal model of a bird, and then suddenly, it was an eagle.

Rusty was pointing up into the air. "That rabbit turned into an eagle and flew away!"

"You're seeing things, too!" I shouted.

The eagle flew off to the left, toward the Woodcraft cabins, and this time, I led the chase with Stipple close behind. The eagle spiraled down near some trees right behind our cabin.

Stipple passed me, and I heard her huffing, "Have to catch the foozlum! Have to catch the foozlum!"

"Wait for me! No fair! Wait for me!" It was ESP's voice coming from far behind us.

We cut across the camp and came out in front of Cabin 3. The tracking device on my wrist was now glowing solid red.

"The foozlum flew in there!" Stipple yelled. "It dove through the open window!"

The horse couldn't fit through the door, so I dove inside. I slammed the door shut behind me, so the thing couldn't escape.

The wrist device was brightest near my bunk. Had the foozlum turned into my bunk? No, of course not. It was under the bunk, where I kept my laptop, so I hauled out my laptop and noticed that my wrist detector was flashing bright red.

I opened the door just as ESP came running up. I held up the laptop. "I've got the foozlum, and now I want my sister back!" I said firmly.

ESP glanced at his own wrist detector, which was also flashing. He switched it off and whirled around to face Stipple. "Human has the foozlum," he remarked disappointedly.

Stipple looked at ESP and gave a kind of horsy shrug. "So it's a draw?" Stipple suggested in a questioning tone.

"A draw," ESP agreed. "This year's hunt-the-foozlum tournament is a draw. Yes!"

I couldn't believe what I had just heard. "Tournament? It's a *game*?"

"It's not just a game. It's *the* game!" Stipple said indignantly. "Ventiri and Saroni were in the tournament playoffs!"

"Foozlum was supposed to land on uninhabited world, not Earth," ESP added unhappily as he shook his head.

"Foozlums have minds of their own, which is what makes foozlum hunting such a great sport," Stipple explained. "When it landed here on Earth, we had no choice but to follow it."

ESP sighed. "We get sister, then you give us foozlum. Nobody will be happy with a draw because now we have to wait for next foozlum season to beat Ventiri."

"Hah!" Stipple snorted, which she did rather emphatically. "Saroni wouldn't stand a chance if you didn't cheat."

"All I want," I said loudly, "is my sister. Work out your game yourselves." I placed the laptop in its carrying case. "Now, take me to Maggie."

"Okay, we get Maggie person," ESP said and Stipple nodded. "Then we go home. If we destroy foozlum before we go, everyone on Earth forgets about us, so it will be no problem."

ESP led us to the tree, but Stipple pushed past him. "You know the rules. We use it during the day and you use it at night, so stand back." Stipple whistled, and the doorway appeared, outlined in a bright blue light.

A second later, Maggie came out, turning to wave at someone behind her that I couldn't see. "Bye! Thanks for the ride!" The door closed and she said, "What's up, Theo? Hey, nice horse."

"You give us foozlum now," ESP said to me.

"I don't think so," I replied and took off running.

I heard Stipple's hoofbeats behind me as I ran. I reached the lake, wound up like a discus thrower, and sent the laptop spiraling through the air. As it made contact, it gave a satisfying splash.

"Foozlum will dissolve in water!" ESP shouted.

"I'm glad to get rid of it," I told them both, and then my head started to feel weird.

ESP reached out and unfastened the—what was it? A wristwatch? The thing on my wrist, anyway. He held it up and said, "No flashes, so foozlum is gone. Yes! I can see their minds, and they are already forgetting about us."

My mind felt foggy. I knew I wanted one thing, though. "Will you aliens please go home now?" I pleaded desperately.

The horse said, "Ventiri Central, extract me from this animal." Then she neighed.

Well, of course she did. Horses . . . can't . . . talk. Can they?

Then the funny-looking kid with greenish hair—what was his name?—well, he waved and walked away.

"What happened?" Maggie asked me as she strolled up to the lake's shore.

"I don't have a clue," I said because I could not remember a thing that happened since lunch.

"I'm so tired, I just want to go to bed."

"Me, too, but I just hope I don't have any strange dreams tonight!" Maggie replied.

I walked Maggie back to her cabin and then continued on to Cabin 3. I was relieved to have this weird day come to an end.

Chapter 8

Show and Tell

By the next morning, even Rusty and Franklin couldn't remember anything about ESP. I was convinced that camp food was making me have strange dreams, and it looked as if the whole experience was going to fade away.

That evening, though, when I looked under my bed, I saw my laptop. I took it out of its case to work on my journal, and something odd happened. The screen lit up and a message appeared that read: *I found my way back to you to say thank you for not destroying me*, and suddenly, all my memory came flooding back. . . .

"I was the only one, though," I finished, with the whole class staring at me. "No one remembered ESP or anything that had happened."

I took a big, deep breath. My throat was dry because I'd been talking for a long, long time. "So, that's what I did on my summer vacation."

No one said anything. Not even Wayne Wilberforce.

Mrs. Gunnarson sighed and shook her head.

"Really, Theodore," she said with a tone of complete exasperation, "I see everyone was right for saying that you have a wonderful imagination. You could grow up to be a marvelous science fiction writer someday."

"Thank you," I said, not quite sure if it was really meant as a compliment.

She raised a finger. "I have to add, though, that I am a bit disappointed, Theodore."

Uh oh, I thought.

"You simply have to learn that real life can be just as interesting as some fantastic tale," Mrs. Gunnarson scolded. "You could easily have told us about what really happened at camp instead of concocting this complicated story."

I picked up my paper bag and said, "I knew you wouldn't believe me."

"How can we believe you?" she asked, her voice kind. "You said your memory had faded, but then you tell us this incredible story."

"The foozlum gave me back my memory because I saved it by throwing my laptop, in its waterproof case, into the lake," I explained.

"There is no such thing as a foozlum, Theodore," Mrs. Gunnarson interrupted curtly. Now she sounded annoyed.

"I knew you'd say that, too," I told Mrs. Gunnarson. The bag started to rattle and rustle, so I held it tightly. I raised my voice above the sound and looked at the class, everyone's eyes fixed on the brown paper bag. "That's why I brought a very special show and tell." Then I released my grip and let the foozlum out of the bag.